CORDELLO

GUIDE TO THE

RUINS OF OSTIA

EDIZIONI STORTI

(Cover) View of the ruins of Ostia Antica

2

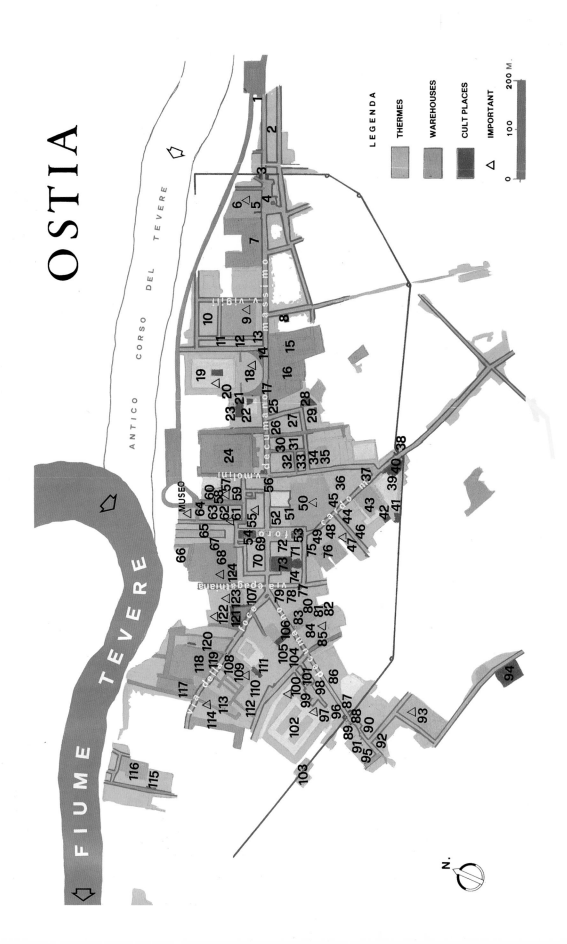

OSTIA

FIUME TEVERE

ANTICO CORSO DEL TEVERE

LEGENDA

THERMES
WAREHOUSES
CULT PLACES
IMPORTANT

0   100   200 M.

N.

78. Macellum
79. Taverns of the Fishmongers
80. Insula of Dionysos
81. Insula of the Eagle
82. Mithraeum of the Seven Doors
83. Baths of the Six Columns
84. Schola of Trajan
85. Narrow Portico of the Windowed Taverns
86. Portico of the Oil Lamp Fountain
87. Caupona of Alexander Helix
88. Marine Gate
89. Sepulchral Monument
90. Sanctuary of the Good Goddess
91. Lightning-Struck Domus
92. Tomb of Cartilius Poplicola
93. Baths of the Marciana
94. Synagogue
95. Domus
96. Domus of the Nymphaeum
97. Domus of the Dioscuri
98. Insula of the Graffito
99. Insula of the Yellow Walls
100. Insula of the Muses
101. Insula of the Painted Vaults
102. Garden Homes
103. Maritime Baths
104. Domus of Mars
105. Temple of the Shipbuilders
106. Christian Basilica
107. House of the Port Mosaic
108. House of Serapis
109. Baths of the Seven Sages
110. House of the Charioteers
111. Chapel of the Three Aisles
112. House of Annius
113. Baths of Trinacria
114. Apartment Building of Serapis and Apartment Building of Bacchus and Ariadne
115. Mithraeum of the Imperial Palace
116. Baths of the Imperial Palace
117. Trajan Markets
118. Horrea of the Wheat Measurers
119. Hall of the Wheat Measurers
120. Baths of Mithra
121. Sacred Area of the Republican Temples
122. Domus of Cupid and Psyche
123. Baths of Buticosus
124. Epagathian and Epafroditian Horrea

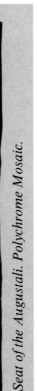

Seat of the Augustali. Polychrome Mosaic.

45. Fullonica
46. Caupona of the Peacock
47. Domus of the Fish
48. Domus of the Columns
49. Nymphaeum of the Erotii
50. Baths of the Forum
51. Forica
52. Apartment Building of the Triclini
53. Capitolium
54. Temple to Rome and Augustus
55. Thermopolium
56. Gate and Wall of the Castrum
57. Apartment Building of the Mill
58. Chapel of Silvanus
59. House of Diana
60. Mithraeum of Lucretius Menander
61. Insula of Jupiter and Ganymede
62. Insula of the Youth Bacchus
63. Insula of the Paintings
64. House of the Dolii
65. Cardo Maximus
66. Apartment Building of the Wheat Measurers
67. Via Tecta
68. Small Market
69. Curia
70. Apartment Building of the Lararium
71. Domus of the Round Temple
72. Basilica
73. Round Temple
74. Collegiate Temple
75. Domus of Jupiter the Fulminator
76. Baths
77. Insula of the Chapel of Isis

MAP OF OSTIA PLACE NAMES

1. Entrance
2. Necropolis on the Via Ostiense
3. Roman Gate and Sullan Wall
4. Square of Victory
5. Republican Warehouses
6. Baths of the Cisiarii
7. Horrea
8. Sabazeum
9. Baths of Neptune
10. Firemen's Barracks
11. Insula of the Child Hercules
12. Insula of the Painted Ceiling
13. Caupona of Fortunatus
14. Christian Memorial
15. Horrea of Hortensius
16. Horrea of Artemis
17. Warehouse of the Dolii and Arcade of the Triumphal Arches
18. Theater
19. Forum of the Corporation
20. Schola of the Sche-Wolf's Altar
21. Domus of Apuleius
22. Four Small Republican Temples
23. Mithraeum of the Seven Spheres
24. Great Horrea
25. Collegiate Temple
26. Seat of the Augustales
27. Fullonica
28. Temple of the Good Goddess
29. Mithraeum of Felixissimus
30. Mithraeum of the Serpents
31. Apartment Building of the Sun
32. Baths
33. Insula of the Envious One
34. Domus of the Provisions Fortune and Domus of the Vestibule
35. Baths
36. Mills
37. Domus of the Medusa
38. Laurentine Gate
39. Temple of Bellona
40. Schola of the Hastiferii
41. Temple of the Great Mother and Sanctuary of Attis
42. Mithraeum of the Animals
43. Baths of the Lightouse
44. Apartment Building of the Child Hercules

Baths of Neptune. Mosaic (det.).

INTRODUCTION

Before beginning the visit to the Ruins of Ostia, it helps knowing some clarifying principles such as to synchronize and predispose spirit and step toward the discovery of a city wherein for centuries the fortunes and misfortunes of Rome were mirrored in equal measure.

Ostia, the city that was *Portus Romae*, domestic landing for Roman cargo boats and warships besides its rich emporium, certainly did not shine by its own light or greatness. Its public and private buildings never matched the splendor of Rome's; nevertheless, to its merit, Ostia didn't have the stench of the squalid slum, and in its massive but sober apartment buildings, for many centuries Ostia's population knew how to live the frugal yet dignified life typical of people devoted to commerce and craftsmanship.

Founded, according to legend, in the remote IV century B.C. by Ancus Martius, Ostia grew constantly until the IV-V century A.D. in an ever faster urban expansion, curiously overlaying within the limited space enclosed by the boundaries of Sulla's city wall new buildings on top of the old, surpassed ones, streets on top of streets, in other words, the imperial city of the II century A.D. on top of the republican city; and then still further restorations, remodelling, readaptation during the late empire on top of the II century A.D. city.

With the fall of the Roman Empire, Ostia ceased its building expansion definitively. In spite of the times, it maintained a dignified aspect, so that Cassiodorus at the beginning of the VI century A.D. defines Ostia and Portus as "two very ornate cities" and Procopius in describing the occupation of Portus made by Vitige in 537 A.D. says, speaking of Ostia, "*city once important, but now lacking all its walls*".

It is certain that the city suffered terrifying invasions and pillages. In the VII century A.D., owing to sacking, even the basilica of St. Aurea was destroyed. In the IX century, in order to somehow come to the aid of the poor, miserable population that still found refuge among the city's ruins or along the coast, Pope Gregory IV built a fortified citadel (*Gregoriopolis*) with the scope of protecting the local inhabitants from raiding by invaders and pirates. For this project, building materials taken from the ruins of Ostia were used.

From that time onward, the city was transformed into an open quarry for valuable building material. For centuries, all those in need drew indiscriminately from there, taking away columns, capitals, statues, bricks, marble, etc. To build their cathedral in the year 1063, the Pisans took large boats down the Tyrrhenian Sea until they came to Ostia and there they took everything they needed; and the cathedral of Orvieto (XIV century) and other buildings in Genoa were built in the same way.

Furnaces for burning marble in order to make it into lime, still identifiable today inside the Baths of Neptune and the Baths of the Seven Sages, sprang up among the ruins of the city.

Tremendous was the spoliation carried out under various popes in order to build the Vatican basilica. The imposing fortress of Ostia begun in 1483 at the will of Cardinal Giuliano della Rovere, later Pope Julius II, was built with Ostia's bricks and with the lime obtained by burning its valuable marble; and likewise the coastal tower called St. Michael's and other minor buildings.

In the XVIII century, given the considerable interest stirred by antique objects, Ostia was subjected to an indiscriminate spoliation on the part of clandestine diggers who alimented collections in half of Europe with their booties. These excavations partially ceased in 1801 when Pope Pius VII prohibited the practice and began regular excavations, but even these had no other purpose than the recovery of art objects.

In 1855, at the will of Pope Pius IX and under the guidance of Ercole Visconti, excavations began, along with restoration of some small, delimited tracts of the city. In 1909, under Dante Vaglieri scientific excavation was begun, along with restoration of that which still was standing in order to preserve it.

Excavations and restorations followed one after another up until 1938 when a grand excavation was begun which had the scope of joining together all zones of the city that previously had been excavated. This project which besides everything else was to give an image of the city as a whole required getting rid of about 600,000 cubic meters of debris. The excavation thus carried out permitted reaching throughout its entire extension the street level the city had at the beginning of the II century A.D. The uncovered area now amounts to about two thirds of the ancient imperial city plan, equivalent to about 340,000 square meters. Il extends for 1,800 meters along the Decumanus Maximus from the Roman Gate down to beyond the Marine Gate, the city's ancient ramification on the sea. At the level of the Forum, the maximum width is 600 meters and it ends in the southwest with the Laurentine Gate.

Proceeding through the city, despite the spoliations there still may be identified 19 thermae, 22 *domus*, 66 *insulae* in 162 apartment buildings, 18 *mithraeums*, 2 mills, 3 laundry-dye shops, 1 theater, besides the temples, warehouses, forums, public and private buildings. The hundreds of taverns along the streets, furthermore, show the vitality of the small businesses which made the city flourish during all those centuries.

CHRONICLE
OF THE CITY
OF OSTIA

CHRONICLE OF THE CITY OF OSTIA

VI century B.C.
According to legend, Ostia was founded by Ancus Martius, IV King of Rome.

IV century B.C.
The *castrum*, fortified citadel, was built in *opus quadratum* in a rectangular form with an area of 14,500 square meters within which modest buildings in *opus incertum* were erected.

III century B.C.
The *castrum* was surrounded by the first living quarters. From the year 267, the Quaestors were instituted and that agglomeration, born spontaneously, was transformed into a true city. Several temples dedicated to Olympic divinities were raised.

II-I century B.C.
There was considerable building expansion, including commercial buildings such as warehouses for commodity storage, living quarters for shopkeepers and artisans and for those who worked in connection with the port, this too presumably created in those early times, and some rich *domus*

87 B.C.
The city was enclosed within a city wall by Sulla.

12 B.C.
The theater was built.

42 A.D. (ca)
The emperor Claudius constructed Ostia's new harbor which was inaugurated afterwards by the emperor Nero in 54 A.D. Claudius also built the Forum of the Corporations, meeting place for all maritime commerce.

60 A.D.
In Nero's age, among other things the large commodities warehouse called the Great *Horrea* was built. After Rome's Great Fire in 64, the emperor Nero ordered that the swamps near the city of Ostia be reclaimed by using the debris from the fire, transported from Rome via the Tiber River by means of cargo ships.

98-117 A.D.
The emperor Trajan enlarged and enriched the Port of Claudius with a large hexagonal dock and enormous warehouses. He had a canal excavated which linked the Tiber with the Port of Claudius and the sea. He constructed other imposing warehouses and public buildings in the city of Ostia.

120 A.D. (ca)
The emperor Hadrian, with a grandiose urban master plan, put the city to an incredible renewal; he tore down entire neighborhoods in order to build there imposing edifices, among which the *Capitolium*, all of the buildings surrounding the Forum, including the thermae, the large residential complex *Homes and Garden*, the *Apartment Buildings of the Charioteers* and *of Serapis*, the *Baths of the Seven Sages*, the enormous *Apartment Building of the Oil Lamp Fountain*, the *Baths of Neptune*, the *Firemen's Barracks*. This restructuring project continued under other emperors for all of the second and part of the third century. In this epoch, many *mithraeums* were built.

312-337 A.D.
The emperor Constantine took away all municipal powers from Ostia, transferring them to the city of Portus.

IV century A.D.
Ostia was embellished by splendid *domus* with rich marble decorations, among which stand out the *Domus of Cupid and Psyche*, the *Domus of the Fish*, the *Domus of the Vestibule*. This is the century in which Ostia's buildings underwent countless restorations and remodelling; but, other than the *domus*, hardly anything new was done.

V century A.D.
Ostia was already well on the way toward decadence.

A hall in the Museum of the excavations

(Above) A statue of Mithra slaying the bull
(Below) Marble group of Cupid and Psyche
P. 11 (Above) Statue of the Emperor Trajan
P. 11 (Below) Statue of Perseus with the head of the Medusa

BRIEF ITINERARY

(Suggested for those who must make a hurried visit).

Starting from the ruins' inside parking lot, visit
the Museum
(60)   the Mithraeum of Lucretius Menandrus
(57)   the Apartment Building of the Mills
(59)   the House of Diana
(61)   the Insula of Jupiter and Ganymede
(55)   the Thermopolium
the Forum
(51)   the Forica
(50)   the Baths of the Forum
(48)   the Domus of the Columns
(34)   the Domus of the Provisions Fortune
(27)   the Fullonica
(26)   the Seat of the Augustales
(18)   the Theater
(19)   the Forum of the Corporations
and from here, return to the parking lot.

THE MUSEUM OF OSTIA

Wanted by Pope Pius IX in 1865 and held in a fourteenth century building previously used as a salt deposit, the Museum of Ostia gathers a fairly good collection of archaeological findings discovered during recent excavations of the city.

Noteworthy is the sculpture collection which boasts statues of very fine workmanship, outstanding among them being the *statue of the emperor Trajan* breast-plated, the *statue of Faustina Major*, the *statue of Cartilius Poplicola*, the *group of Mithra* while killing the bull, the *statue of Perseus with Medusa's head*, and the *statue of Julia Domna Diva*. The portrait collection enumerates personages of Ostia, of the imperial family, and philosophers, among which are the *portrait bust of Volcacius Miropnous*, the *head of Trajan*, the *portrait of Faustina Major*, and the *portrait bust of Asclepius*. Small marble groups such as *The Thorn Extractor* and *Cupid and Psyche* merit attention. There are, among other things, a collection of sarcophagi and excellent bas-reliefs, examples of wall paintings taken from tombs, emblems in polychrome mosaic, and an excellent example of polychrome *opus sectile* with what is presumed to be the *portrait of Christ giving the benediction*.

A minor collection of bronzes, antique artisan objects, oil lamps, and glassware should not be forgotten. In a small room are gathered several molded clay reliefs and several shop signs. Among the curiosities shown in the museum, there is a marble slab upon which two pairs of feet have been carved opposite one another; it was found in the Temple of Bellona, goddess of war, where probably a soldier who had left for war and had come back safe and sound had made a gift of it in thanksgiving as an explicit votive act.

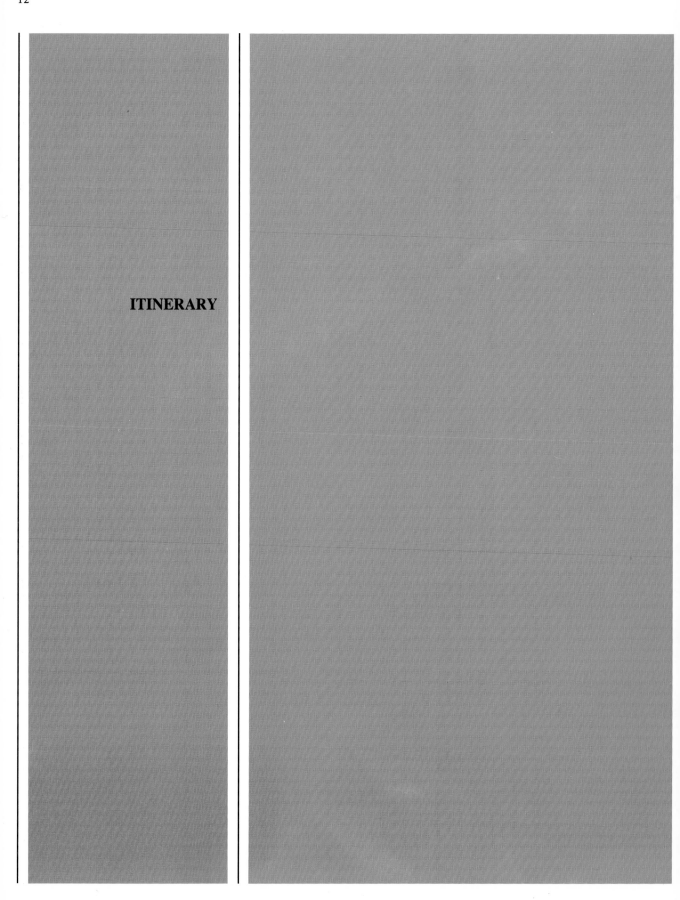

ITINERARY

ITINERARY

1. **Entrance**
2. **Necropolis**
   on the Via Ostiense

Once beyond the entrance to the Ruins of Ostia (1), the first physical contact that one has with the ruins is that with the flagstones of the Via Ostiense along which extends a short tract of the ancient necropolis (2).

Remains of tombs that once were adorned with rich architectural decorations and that now appear miserably barren in their wall structure show, besides the wear of time, that unceasing clandestine activity carried out through all of the past centuries by inexperienced diggers in search of valuable funeral layouts or wonderful treasures. Notwithstanding the spoliation, it is still possible to identify in those structures the essential outlines of the family tombs of Ostia's well-to-do citizens. Advancing along the Via Ostiense or going to the left of it where another flagstone street runs parallel, one may recognise *arcosolium*-style tombs from the late empire and more antique columbaria where urns (terra-cotta containers for ashes) were placed in small niches made in the walls. A few fragments of marble or terra-cotta sarcophagi together with fragments of funeral inscriptions scattered here and there remain scanty witnesses of burials. These end just outside of the city walls (Sullan Wall-3) which drastically divided the city's space from the necropolis.

3. Roman gate and Sullan Wall

Leaving the necropolis, one comes before the remains of the Roman Gate. The Via Ostiense ends here, changing to the Decumanus Maximus on the other side of the gate. A pedestal set to the right was the base of a statue of some magnanimous Roman emperor. The gate rises from a lower level, that of the ancient urban level of the I century B.C. Large blocks of tufa from the *opus quadratum* that constituted the wall structure outline the advanced part of one of the two towers. In the middle, the barrel vaulted gate let one into the city. Two *winged Minervas*, one of which is placed in the inner square called Victory (4), probably decorated the façade. An inscription placed in the same square records the ancient restorations of the wall and of the gate itself.

To the sides of the gate, one may still note traces of the nucleus of the masonry that made up the Sullan Wall built between 82 and 79 B.C., now visible only along several short tracts. The part that has been excavated of the wall that enclosed the city on its southeast side measures 1840 meters.

Once through the gate, a large square, where remains of a large pool or fountain stand out to the left, permitted the *cisiarii* (cart drivers) who were also in charge of the service between Ostia and Rome to stop and park. On the right side of the square, a large warehouse (5) from the republican period, in which one may note both the columnar portico and several rooms, precedes the fine Roman bath complex of the *cisiarii* (6).

P. 13 (Above) Roman Gate Necropolis. Columbarium.
P. 13 (Below) Roman Gate Necropolis. Cornice of a tomb door.
Roman Gate. Winged Minerva.

6. Baths of the Cisiarii

Roman bath complex dating back to the end of the I-beginning of the II century A.D., it was built upon the ruins of precedent provision warehouses. Probably owned by the Corporation of the *Cisiarii*, it still preserves, even though grossly restored in the III century, the *frigidarium's* fine square *mosaic*, 8.70 meters each side, which reproduces the typical activities of this corporation. All around a turreted citadel there are inserted small scenes of the cart drivers' activities. Another city wall encloses and borders the mosaic.

It is thought that the *cisiarii*, besides offering urban public service, united Ostia and Rome as well along the Via Ostiense in a quite rapid service with both the *cisium*, two-wheeled cart for carrying passengers, and the *carruca*, four-wheeled one for carrying merchandise and baggage.

Going back to the Decumanus from the baths and heading toward the center of the city, one passes by an enormous, partially excavated *warehouse* (7) dating back to the time of the emperor Antoninus Pius. Several grates in the flagstoning of the Decumanus let one glimpse the lead tubing of Ostia's aqueduct. A medieval well built right in the middle of the street is evidence of the presence of a community in Ostia even at that time. On the right is the great columnar portico that announces the Baths of Neptune (9).

Roman Gate. Pedestal for an emperor's statue.
Baths of the Cisiarii. Mosaic of the frigidarium.

9. Baths of Neptune

Grandiose complex of Roman baths begun at the time of Hadrian and then suspended for lack of funds (an inscription reveals that the emperor Antoninus Pius granted Ostia's inhabitants the funds needed to complete the edifice, finishing it thus at his own expense in 139 A.D.), it arises upon the ruins of pre-existing buildings also used as Roman baths. The well divided, functional building still has one of the most grandiose mosaics as for composition in Ostia. In an 18 x 12 meter space in the main room is represented the *Triumph of Neptune*. Driving four pawing seahorses, he is encircled by a procession of sea monsters, Nereids, and Tritons. The mosaic of the adjacent room represents the queen of the sea, Amphitrite, driven by Hymen and four Tritons (one of which is no longer visible) who play cymbals and *kantharos*. On the right side of the room in an area now covered by roofing is found one of the many lime furnaces set up in the city during the Middle Ages for burning marble to make it into lime.

Entering the building by way of the Via dei Vigili, one can identify a room heated by pipes set inside the walls (*laconicum*) and the *calidarium* with the *praefurnia* system. A large gymnasium used for athletic excercises conceals beneath its floor a tank for water divided into six long sections covered by barrel vaults. Following a terrible fire that seriously damaged them, the baths were restored under Marcus Aurelius. Other restorations in the wall structure date back to the IV century A.D.

Leaving the baths, it is advisable to proceed along the Via dei Vigili.

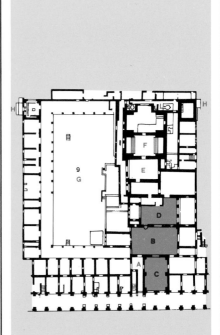

BATHS OF NEPTUNE

A - Small terrace with panoramic view
B - Mosaic of Neptune
C - Mosaic of Amphitrite
D - Frigidarium
E - Laconicum
F - Calidarium
G - Gymnastics field
H - Cisterns
I - Praefurnium
L - Boilers

Blue - Mosaic

P. 16 Baths of Neptune. Mosaic of Amphitrite.
(Above) Baths of Neptune. Gymnasium.
(Below) Baths of Neptune. Rooms of the frigidarium.

10. Firemen's Barracks

Before getting to the Firemen's Barracks, one comes to a cistern along the street that is named after it. A little farther ahead, beneath the street level lies a fine black and white *mosaic floor* which was part of a building from Claudius' age destroyed by Hadrian in order to make way for the new installations of the Baths of Neptune and of the Firemen's Barracks. The mosaic illustrates, among other things, some Roman provinces symbolized by portraits of women: Sicily, Africa, Spain, and Egypt.

Built at the time of Hadrian in 132 A.D., the Firemen's Barracks were the seat of a corps of cohorts detached from Rome with firemen's duties (an institution going back to the time of Claudius). Before crossing the main entrance of the barracks, one may note the remains of mosaic flooring in two small wine shops probably reserved for the troops.

On the inside, a two-story porticoed court divided the rooms set aside for the troops and services. On the wall of the latrine to the left is a small tabernacle dedicated to the sacred fortune. In 207 A.D., an *augusteum* was made inside of the portico for the emperors' cult (very much followed by the military). Some bases which held statues of deified emperors decorate the room in back. The bases used for those of Severus, Caracalla, and Julia Domna are identifiable. A black and white mosaic representing a scene of sacrifice floored the hall of the *augusteum*.

Having left the barracks, one heads toward the *Insula of the Child Hercules* (11).

(Above) Firemen's Barracks. Court.
(Below) Via della Caserma dei Vigili.
Remains of a pre-Hadrian building.
P. 19 (Above) Firemen's Barracks.
Detail of the mosaic of the Augusteum.
P. 19 (Below) Via della Caserma dei Vigili. Cistern.

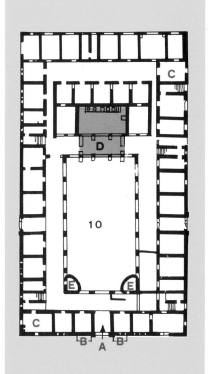

FIREMEN'S BARRACKS

A - Main entrance
B - Wine shops
C - Foricae
D - Augusteum: mosaic with scene
    of sacrifice
E - Cisterns

Blue - Mosaic

11. **Insula
of the Child Hercules**
12. **Insula
of the Painted Ceiling**
13. **Caupona of Fortunatus**

Along the Via della Cisterna stands a large apartment building, it too dating back to the time of Hadrian, which is composed on the ground floor of two *insulae*; some flights of stairs are proof of at least a second floor. In both *insulae* one senses the well-being of their inhabitants who must have belonged to the middle class, probably dedicated to maritime activities.
In the *Insula of the Child Hercules* (11), some remains of wall painting reveal the sobriety of the decorations, characterized by simple squares of color with rare figuration and in some cases small checks or small figures wandering in a vast background. The pictorial decoration is kept along these lines in other contemporary rich *insulae* as well.
The Via della Cisterna is closed near the Decumanus by a late *caupona* (13) with a mosaic floor.

14. Christian memorial

Set to the side of one of the two *nymphaeums* that frame the theater along the Decumanus, one may identify the memorial that honors Ostia's III century Christian martyrs. Among those known best, Aurea, to whom the basilica built in the necropolis of the Via Ostiense and erected above her tomb was later dedicated (the present church of Ostia Antica), and the martyrs Cyriac, Hyppolitus, Asterius, Prepedigna should be remembered. The sarcophagus with the effigy of Orpheus is supposed to have held the mortal remains of the bishop Cyriac. Also honored is St. Monica who died in the city of Ostia while waiting to embark for Africa.
Ostia's Christian community must have been numerous and very active, despite the scarse information which has come down to us, if as St. Augustine mentions "*it was the most famous among Rome's outlying sees*" and "*the bishop of Ostia from time immemorial has the right to consecrate the one elected to St.*

Peter's cathedra". Considerable traces of Christian life still appear among the ruins. Christian symbols decorate many buildings. Fish, doves, and chalices are variously represented in mosaic or in sculpture as a votive act. Christian oil lamps have been found among the ruins of the city.
On the left side of the Decumanus, the great *Horrea* of *Hortensius* (15) looms.

15. **Horrea of Hortensius**
16. **Horrea of Artemis**
17. **Warehouse of the Dolii
behind the Arcade
of the Triumphal Arches**

This is a large group of provision warehouses of which the most antique is the *Horrea* of Hortensius (15) dating back to the I century B.C.. The floor of the *horrea*, unlike the other two, appears lower since the republican street level was in use at that time.
In the III century, a chapel dedicated to an unknown divinity was built

(Left) The cistern from which the street gets its name.
(Right) Nymphaeum on the Decumanus and Christian Memorial.
P. 21 (Above left) Cornice of the Portico of the Triumphal Arches.
P. 21 (Above right) Capital on the Portico of the Triumphal Arches.
P. 21 (Below) Horrea of Hortesius. Panoramic view.

on the right edge of the columnar portico.

The *Horrea* of Artemis (16) are composed, among other things, of a notable deposit of buried *dolii*, used for keeping wine or oil.

All of them underwent restorations at the time of Marcus Aurelius.

According to the *Liber Pontificalis*, in front of the theater on the Decumanus were erected one or more triumphal arches, under one of which St. Aurea, St. Cyriac, and some of their companions suffered martyrdom; however, there is no trace of them. Only a fine corbel, a fragment of cornice, and a capital remain which are now on display along the portico called precisely of the Triumphal Arches (17).

18. Theater

Built in 12 B.C. at the time of Augustus in blocks of tufa, it was enlarged and restructured in 196 A.D. in order to increase its capacity. It was faced and adorned in its columnar arcades with brick pilasters and the large central entrance was adorned with valuable stucco work. Its capacity was thus brought to 3500. A wide gallery made with veined marble columns decorated the high part of the seating bowl. (Some of these columns are now on the back of the stage and along the Decumanus near the Christian Memorial (14)). The permanent scenery at the back of the stage, originally rising three architectonic orders high, is now totally lacking. Some fragments of it together with three theatrical masks are fastened to the two tufa walls of the proscenium.

During the late empire, it underwent new restorations and also was stuccoed and painted. Traces of this antique restoration may be noted in the fallen fragments along the Via delle Corporazioni. It was also adapted for acquatic shows by flooding the low zone called orchestra. The necessary water was collected in two large cisterns set up in the two front taverns facing the Decumanus.

Brought to light and restored in the first half of our century, it hosts classical theatrical shows during the summer season.

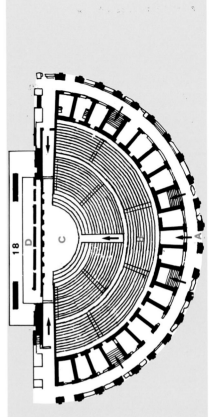

THEATER

A - Main entrance
B - Seating bowl
C - Orchestra
D - Stage

P. 22 (Below left) Forum of the Corporations. Altar of Romulus and Remus.
P. 22 (Above) Theater. Fragment of an arch on the Via delle Corporazioni.
P. 22 (Below) Theater. Theatrical masks.
(Above) Theater. Façade on the Decumanus.
(Below) Theater. Seating bowl.

19. Forum of the Corporations

Built at the time of Claudius, the great quadrangular portico with two rows of brick Doric columns was used to hold the seats of the commercial and maritime *stationes* in 50 offices. A triumphal entrance to the forum made of pillared arches opened on the north side opposite the theater. Center of Ostia's commercial life, the forum was where all business connected with maritime affairs was conducted.

With the enlargement of the theater in 196 A.D., the portico underwent changes and restorations which, besides raising the floor 40 centimeters, widened the space in the arcade, bringing the original 50 *stationes* up to 64.

The mosaic inscriptions specified and publicized the various commercial and maritime activities in which each *statio* dealt. The ships reproduced in the mosaics are cargo ships used for transporting merchandise from all of the supply centers scattered around the Mediterranean basin.

Rising on a high podium in the middle of the forum and encircled by cippi and monuments of Ostia's worthy citizens is the temple, perhaps dedicated to Ceres, where traders probably went to make offerings after having made a good business deal at the forum.

21. Domus of Apuleius

The *domus* was probably built about the middle of the I century A.D. in an L-shaped space which on the north winds around the podium of the *Four Small Republican Temples* (22). It gets its name from an inscription found on a leaden pipe: Apuleius Marcellus. It has a columnar atrium encircled by small rooms decorated with black and white mosaic floors. Various restorations which supposedly date back to the II and III centuries A.D. changed the rooms and floors.

It borders the *Mithraeum of the Seven Spheres* (23) on the west.

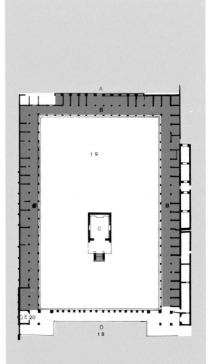

22. Four small Republican Temples

Modest remains of four small republican temples rise upon a single high podium in blocks of tufa. One can make out the walls of the cells and several fragments of the column's bases. They appear structurally different even though of equal dimensions. They probably were dedicated to four different Olympic divinities. A grassy square reveals the ancient urban level of the republican period.

23. Mithraeum of the Seven Spheres

It is one of the best preserved of Ostia's 18 *mithraeums*; it dates back to the III century A.D. and clearly shows some of the structural characteristics that distinguish all of Ostia's *mithraeums*. The room is a long, narrow rectangular area divided into three parts: two *podia* (bench-like constructions) and a corridor. The two *podia* served for holding the faithful who partecipated in the rite; the corridor led to the sacrificial altar and to another where the image of the god Mithra was placed.

The *podia* and the floor of the corridor are decorated in black and white mosaic. Delineated on the floor are seven semicircles in progressive order going toward the altar signifying the seven celestial spheres or the seven phases necessary in order to reach knowledge. It should be noted in connection with this that the number seven is recurrent in almost all of Ostia's *mithraeums* even though it is variously represented in the mosaics. To the sides of the podia are symbols of the zodiac and other figures.

Other *mithraeums* worth visiting are: the *Mithraeum of Felicissimus* (29) which has objects symbolizing the various stages of the cult in the mosaic floor of its corridor; the *Mithraeum of Lucretius Menandrus* (60), this, too, in excellent condition; the *Mithraeum of the Animals* (42); the *Mithraeum of the Seven Doors* (82) where a splendid garden is represented in a fresco on one of the side walls.

Moreover, it should be noted that in the museum a very beautiful marble group is displayed which comes from the *mithraeum* of the baths by the same name (120) and represents Mithra while he is killing a bull.

FORUM OF THE CORPORATIONS

A - Ancient entrance to the Forum
B - Mosaics of the stationes
C - Temple of Ceres
D - Theater stage
E - Altar of the She-Wolf and twins

Blu - Mosaico

P. 24 (Above) Forum of the Corporations. Temple of Ceres.
P. 24 (Below) Forum of the Corporations. Left side of the portico.
Forum of the Corporations. Statio with the scene in mosaic of transshipping commodities.

24. Great Horrea

These impressive warehouses rising not far from the Forum of the Corporations were built in the I century A.D. in the period that goes from Claudius to Nero. Majestic in size, they also are perhaps the most interesting from the point of view of their structure. Always used as cereal warehouses, it is possible to notice under the floors of some of the cells the great space which was left so as to allow an excellent isolation and thus a satisfactory defense against humidity.

The warehouses operated for a long time; restorations dating back to the IV century A.D. confirm it.

25. Collegiate Temple

Built by one of the many craft corporations operating in the harbor city, it is made within an enclosed, reserved area since it was set aside for the cult of the *sodales*, that is, members of the college. Several rooms precede the court of the temple of which the steps and the high podium remain. A marble fragment of the pediment with traces of bas-reliefs is set on the surrounding wall that faces the Decumanus Maximus.

26. Seat of the Augustales

Edifice dating back to the second half of the II century A.D., it is made on top of a precedent building complex dating back to the republican period. It was the political-religious collegial seat of the Augustales (those in charge of taking care of the cult of emperors).

The main entrance opening onto the Decumanus leads into a porticoed court which is embellished by a pretty fountain; around the portico, small rooms and a lovely apsidal hall decorated in the late empire with polychrome marble slabs. The statue that is thought to represent the emperor Maxentius as maximum pontifex and which is now on display in the museum was found among other statues representing members of the imperial family during excavations in this hall. In the small room to the right, there is a black and white *mosaic* with a polychrome emblem representing two winged cupids at the center.

The Seat of the Augustales appears to have been restored and enlarged in a very late epoch. That proves how, even during the late empire and with the prevailing of Christianity and the oriental cults, the glorification of personages of the imperial house persisted tenaciously among vast strata of the population.

Seat of the Augustales with copy of a woman's statue.

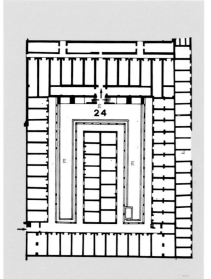

GREAT HORREA
E - Porticoed court

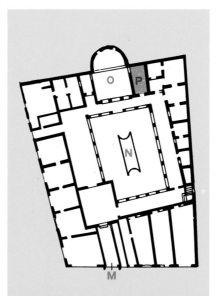

SEAT OF THE AUGUSTALES
M - Main entrance on the Decumanus
N - Fountain
O - Triclinium
P - Room with polychrome mosaic

Blue - Mosaic

27. Fullonica

Ancient laundry-dye shop, structurally it is made up of several large basins containing the water needed for the various operations; all around the room, small terra-cotta tubs where the *fullones* (those in charge of the laundry) did the washing and coloring of materials.

Among the many laws that guaranteed order and cleanliness in the Roman streets, there was one that allowed cleaners to hang their materials out to dry along the street without having to pay sanctions.

Another large *fullonica*, not as well preserved, is found along the Via delle Corporazioni and a smaller one along the Cardo Maximus (45).

28. Temple of the Good Goddess
29. Mithraeum of Felixissimus

Once past the *fullonica*, at the end of the Via degli Augustali one can glimpse a group of buildings in *opus reticolatum* rising from an urban level much lower than the street. The complex, dating from the I century B.C., includes the Temple of the Good Goddess (28) of which remain only low structures of the cells and the adjacent rooms used for living quarters and services for the vestals. An altar in front of the temple and a well complete the structures. The whole is enclosed by a high wall which isolated the sacred area of the goddess from indiscreet glances.

The Good Goddess was venerated by women who invoked fertility and harvest protection from her.

To the right of the wall enclosing the area dedicated to the Good Goddess lies the small *Mithraeum* of Felixissimus (29) of which the design of the corridor's mosaic floor is still visible.

30. **Mithraeum of the Serpents**
31. **Apartment building of the Sun**
32. **Baths**
33. **Insula of the Envious One**

Going along the Via della Fortuna Annonaria, before reaching the house by the same name one comes to a small street on the right called Via del Caseggiato del Sole. It divides two blocks of buildings dating back to the age of Antoninus Pius which extend as far as the Decumanus Maximus. The first to the right (31) includes a series of shops and homes where there is still evidence of wall paintings, besides the *Mithraeum* of the Serpents (30). In the block to the left, instead, there is the *Insula* of the Envious One (33), so called because of the showy inscription on the mosaic floor.

34. **Domus**
    of the Provisions Fortune
    Domus of the Vestibule
36. **Mills**
37. **Domus of the Medusa**

Following first the Via della Fortuna Annonaria and then the street named Semita dei Cippi, one may admire among other things three lovely *domus* of the III-IV century A.D.
The first, called *Domus* of the Provisions Fortune, besides a fine columnar peristyle, still has a room floored with a black and white mosaic reproducing in octagonal spaces representations of mythical personages, among which the Capitoline She-Wolf with twins stands out. On the opposite side, an absidal hall with a graceful *nymphaeum* reveals traces of valuable African marble facing. A small door leads from the room into a space beneath the staircase where room had been made for a single latrine.
Moving along toward the Laurentine Gate, on the left one finds the *Domus* of the Vestibule which welcomes one into its hallway with a beautiful polychrome mosaic made up of very large marble tesserae. An ancient restoration closed the entrance of the porticoed peristyle in order to put a fountain with niches there. All around there are rooms and the staircase that led to the up-

A - Domus of the Provisions Fortune
B - Domus of the Vestibule

Blue - Mosaic

per floor. It is interesting to note in this *domus* a small *nymphaeum* made under the peristyle; it may be reached by means of a few steps to the right of the arcade. Small niches and a very narrow passageway lead into a narrow room where there is a well.

Returning to the street, on the right we find a mill which preserves its fine millstones.

A little farther ahead is the trapezoidal *Domus* of the Medusa. This small, strange *domus* has the peculiarity of its rooms being small and trapezoidal, with black and white mosaics reproducing *Gorgons*.

38. Laurentine Gate
39. Temple of Bellona
40. Schola of the Hastiferii
41. Temple of the Great Mother
    Sanctuary of Attis

The Laurentine Gate, so called because it put one onto the road that led to Laurentum, is still visible in part of one of the two towers in *opus quadratum* and a fair stretch of the Sullan Wall. It, too, set on the lower I century B.C. street level, now appears to lean upon and be overcome by the II-III century A.D. constructions.

About a hundred meters outside of the gate lies a rich necropolis called *of the Claudii* of which a brief tract in proximity of the Via del Mare has been excavated and restored. The inside part of the gate, together with the walls of the Sullan Wall, the Baths of the Lighthouse, and the Cardo Maximus, forms a triangular space called Field of the Great Mother where several temples and places of worship dating back to the II-III century A.D. are sited.

Built against the old gate is the Temple of Bellona (39), goddess of war. It is preceded by an enclosure and a room set aside for the Schola of the Hastiferii (40). The members of this college had the duty of looking after and conducting the cerimonies of the war goddess' cult. Women were severely prohibited from entering this place. During the Other small chapels occupy the area; among them, the Sanctuary of Attis, preceded by two fine telamones in the guise of Pan. Here, the oriental cults, which especially in the III century A.D. dominated the city chronicles with their sumptuous, picturesque rites, found their place. At the back of the vertex of the open space rises the podium and part of the wall of the cell of the Temple of the Magna Mater which enjoyed a considerable following among Ostia's inhabitants.

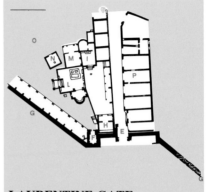

LAURENTINE GATE
E - Gate
F - Tower in opus quadratum
G - Sullan Wall
H - Temple of Bellona
I - Schola of the Hastiferii
L - Sanctuary of Attis
M - Sacellum
N - Sacellum
O - Field of the Great Mother
P - Tavern

P. 27 (Above) Fullonica on the Cardo Maximus.
P. 27 (Below) Fullonica on the Via degli Augustali.
P. 27 (Below right) Mithraeum of Felixissimus. Floor mosaic.
P. 28 (Above) Domus of the Provisions Fortune. Room with nymphaeum.

P. 28 (Below) Domus of the Provisions Fortune. Forica.
(Left) Necropolis of the Claudii. Sanctuary of Attis. Front.

43. Baths of the Lighthouse

Built in Hadrian's time, the edifice has undergone various changes and restorations. Upon entering there, one finds a tavern with a fine counter covered with polychrome marbles; several meters ahead on the left, the *frigidarium* with a curious black and white mosaic where what is probably Ostia's lighthouse is represented in the midst of a sea full of fish and sea monsters with heads the shape of a ram, a bull, a lioness, a griffin, etc.
A room roofed over after restorations holds a basin faced in marble and a fresco representing a Nereid on a bull. Interesting are the various superimpositions of layers of plaster on the same wall which show the different remodelling and the long life that the Roman bath complex enjoyed.

46. Caupona of the Peacock

It gets its name from the figure of a peacock painted in a niche. This is one of the rare tavern-lodges identified for certain in Ostia. Adapted for the purpose towards the III century A.D. from a pre-existing building, it is divided into two stories. On the first floor, right after the entrance, one notices a small latrine; a little farther ahead on the right, quite a nice room decorated with a fresco where a bar and shelves for displaying food stand out. A small door leads into a tiny room decorated with a fresco having figures representing the muses. A small outside court with a counter that went around it seated clients. The upper floor was used for lodging.

Considering that Ostia was a harbor city, the scarceness of places like this is surprising, although as many ancient authors remind us, these were frequented only by the lowest classes of the population since the wealthy and the noble were guests in the city's rich *domus* or *insulae* when travelling and hosts of servants looked after their every need during the journey. Pliny, speaking of these places, recalls that they were full of summer bugs, that they gave forth unbearable cooking odors, and that the mattresses were filled with reed leaves instead of feathers; on the other hand, the prices were reasonable. Of course, not all inns were so horrible and the *Caupona* of the Peacock seems to prove it.

47. Domus of the Fish
48. Domus of the Columns
49. Nymphaeum of the Erotii

Two late *domus* appear along the Via della Caupona del Pavone: the *Domus* of the Fish (47) and the *Domus* of the Columns (48). Both having come into being toward the end of the III century, they underwent fairly major remodelling and restoration in the second half of the IV century A.D.
Interesting is the triclinium of the *Domus of the Fish,* floored with a black and white *mosaic* reproducing various squares and symbols. Several late basins decorate the columnar peristyle onto which faces a small room, now covered by roofing, which boasts a fairly good floor in polychrome *opus sectile* that reproduces marble panels inlaid with Maltese crosses. The house's small entrance is decorated with a polychrome mosaic in the center of which are a chalice and a fish. These symbols make it presumable that the house belonged to some rich Christian family.
The *Domus* of the Columns is decorated with a mosaic floor made of large polychrome tesserae, typical of the flooring technique used in the late empire. The main entrance

to the *domus* opens onto the Cardo Maximus where a little farther ahead there is a luminous *nymphaeum* called "**of the Erotii**" (49), this, too, built in the same epoch. The floor of the *nymphaeum* as well as its walls with the lovely columnar niches are decorated with precious marbles. The center of the *nymphaeum* is occupied by a pretty, very well preserved pool.

50. Baths of the Forum

Looking onto the forum from the east is the great complex called *Baths of the Forum*. They are the largest in Ostia. Built in the II century A.D., they show innumerable restorations carried out during the late empire. A large trapezoidal gym surrounded by porticoes and paved with mosaic closed about the imposing structures that faced southeast with the elliptical *laconicum* (steam baths) and *calidarium* (hot water baths). Great windows lighted the room. An underground passage winding through the building's complex structure allowed the baths' attendants to take care of lighting the boilers and emptying the pools in order to change the water. Making one's way along that passage, it is possible to note the furnaces under the rooms' flooring and the *hypocausta* wherein the heat was channeled. Remains of the piping laid in the walls document that ingenious heating system. The bases of four large boilers that were used to produce boiling water and steam are visible on the northeast side of the edifice. The *frigidarium* (cold water baths) was in the immense, richly decorated hall, of which remain as last witnesses several fragments of veined marble columns and a corbel of the rich cornice that decorated the level where the vault began.

P. 30 (Left) Baths of the Lighthouse. Frigidarium.
P. 30 (Right) Domus of the Fish. Mosaic.
(Above) Nymphaeum of the Erotii. Fountain.
(Below) Baths of the Forum. View of the gymnastics field.

51. Forica
52. Apartment building of the Triclinia

Although the *forica* (latrine) is in the Apartment Building of the Triclinia, it was for the use of passers-by. Its sewer system was in common with another inside latrine in the apartment building. A long bench with twenty holes that went all along the walls welcomed the wayfarers. A small water drain allowed greater hygiene. The two small doors that faced the street connecting the forum with a small square called «Forum of the Heroic Statue» were pivoted at the middle of the threshold so that turning on themselves they offered a minimum of privacy (A).

The apartment building, also built by Hadrian in 120-125 A.D., has the peculiarity of having all of the rooms going along the right of the inside portico used as triclinia. The *podia* where the table companions took their places are still visible.

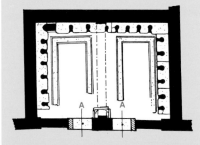

A - Revolving doors

APARTMENT BUILDING OF THE TRICLINIA
A - Entrance
B - Triclinia
C - Forica

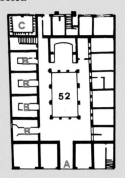

Forum
53. Capitolium
**54. Temple
to Rome and Augustus**

The Forum, center of the city's religious-political life and throbbing heart of its various daily activities, was made by knocking down many of the old structures that were an integral part of the old *castrum* and of which modest remains are left. Rectangular like all Latin forums, it was projected as early as 20-25 A.D., period in which the Temple of Rome and Augustus was built.

At the same time or shortly after, the basilica and the curia, seat of Ostia's senate, also were built. Only in the years around 125 A.D. did Hadrian, after demolishing a small precedent temple, build in its place the grandiose *Capitolium* flanked by two long columnar porticoes which served to hold citizens on rainy days.

The *Capitolium*, dedicated to the Capitoline triad Jupiter, Juno, and Minerva, was completely faced with precious marbles. It is still possible to single out the holes left by the bronze clamps in the brick walls. Some fragments of the temple's pe-

diment are now visible on the wall that delimits the portico on the right. Remains of the large quadrangular cell with its high niches have always soared above the heap of ruins into which the city had fallen. Chronicles of the time reveal that at the beginning of the year 1700, that place was used by the local shepherds as a large sheepfold and was identified as "the red house".

Of the older Temple of Rome and Augustus remain the podium's foundations and the fine marble façade reassembled on the modern wall built to the side.

P. 32 (Above) House of Diana.
P. 32 (Center) Apartment Building of the Triclinia. Forica.
P. 32 (Below left) Capitolium. Remains of the cornice.
P. 32 (Below right) Forum. Remains of the marble decoration of the Temple of Rome and Augustus.
(Above) Capitolium. Front.
(Below) Forum. Remains of the Temple of Rome and Augustus.

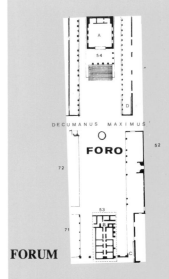

FORUM

A - Capitolium
B - Temple of Rome and Augustus
C - Remains of the marble decoration of the Temple of Rome and Augustus
D - Remains of the marble decoration of the Capitolium

55. Thermopolium

The fine apartment building that stands out on the left side of the Via della Casa di Diana still shows us the wooden balconies of the second floor where the ancient inhabitants of Ostia loved to linger outside on sultry summer evenings. A little farther on, a balconied gallery juts out which with three barrel vaults frames the entrances to the *Thermopolium* (55), ancient bar-snack room. The apartment building and the snack bar date back to 125 A.D., but they underwent innumerable restorations during the late empire.

A fine marble counter stands out at the entrance to the ancient bar in such a way so that the clients who were in a hurry could come up to it from the street and the others could come to it from inside the bar. Hot and cold food and drink were served there; other than cool cellar wine, among the better known dishes served were hot wine with honey, pizzas made out of legume flours,

and sausages. The finely frescoed central room has a still life above a counter with shelves which probably illustrates the food then in vogue. In the room to the right, a small oven shows the frugality with which hot food was prepared. A large buried *dolium* was perhaps used to hold oil for frying. The room to the left, paved with a little fountain and a long counter welcomed clients in good weather. A short staircase led to a small cellar.

56. Gate and wall of the castrum

Built around the end of the IV century B.C. in tufa in *opus quadratum*, the *castrum* is rectangular in shape and measures 194 × 125,70 meters. Four single-fornix gates opened up, one at the center of each side. Two streets (the Decumanus Maximus and the Cardo Maximus) crossed each other at the center, dividing the area inside into four equal parts. The ancient Via

Ostiense, still visible, went as far as the *castrum*'s east gate; from that point onward, it became the Decumanus Maximus. At the *castrum*'s center where the massive *Capitolium* now rises, in an open trench it is still possible to see the remains of the flagstone of the old Cardo and structures in tufa of the ancient republican constructions.

Created as a necessary defense of the Tiber's mouth and as Rome's military ramification on the coast, the *castrum* was very soon surrounded by a populated area which had already begun to develop in the III century B.C. Between the middle of the II and the I century B.C., commercial buildings and luxurious *domus* with atrium and peristyle rose and multiplied. Its function as a fortified citadel thus died out completely and many of the buildings that were built later on incorporated or were leaned against those ancient walls themselves.

57. Apartment building of the Mill
58. Chapel of Sylvanus
59. House of Diana
60. Mithraeum
 of Lucretius Menandrus

The building called *House of Diana* (59) is of particular interest. Originally spread out on three or four stories, it probably rose 18 meters high, the maximum height permitted civil constructions by Roman laws of Trajan's time. Built about 130-140 A.D., it represents the typical *insula* made up of various apartments (*cenacula*) which the owner (*dominus insulae*) rented to tenants. The first floor consists of taverns with mezzanines, the latter being rooms where shopkeepers and the lower class of the population lived. Stairways led to the upper floors where partitionings outline, instead, comfortable apartments for the middle class. A balcony went around the building on the second floor.

Entering the first floor corridor, one notes a room to the right in the back that was used in ancient times as a latrine. Farther ahead on the left is the building's quadrangular court which held a cistern and a pool for the tenants' use. On the wall to the left, a clay tablet representing the *Huntress Diana* gives the house its name. In the dark end of the room to the north, a modest *mithraeum* was made, of which two *podia* for the faithful and an altar where the image of the god Mithra was placed can be seen.

Built against the right side of the House of Diana is its contemporary apartment building called of the Mill (57) where millstones and several oil presses are still in place in a large room. The millstones were made out of blocks of lava and were set in motion by mules yoked to the movable upper part. The mill seems to be connected with two taverns facing the Via della Casa di Diana; thus it is probable that those taverns were used for selling flour as well as the bread made and baked in the rooms in back of the mill itself. Between the two buildings, there is a small chapel called of Silvanus (58) where traces of wall painting from a fresco are still preserved.

On the northwest side of the two apartment buildings, one comes to a lovely house which holds a well preserved *mithraeum* called of Lucretius Menandrus (60).

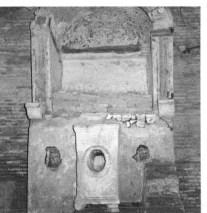

P. 34 (Above left) Mural painting (det.).
(Below left) Murll painting (det.).
(Above right) Thermopolium. *Interior.*
(Below right) Thermopolium. *The Façade.*
P. 35 (Above left) House of Diana. Cistern in the Court.
(Above right) Apartment Buildings of the Mills. Millstones.
(Below left) Western Entrance of the Castrum.
(Below right) House of Diana. Altar in the mithraeum.

Apartment building with:

61. **Insula of Jupiter and Ganymede**
62. **Insula of the Youth Bacchus**
63. **Insula of the Paintings**
64. **House of the Dolii**

This is one of the most varied of the *insula*-type apartment buildings that Ostia has. Erected on top of a precedent building that was demolished down to street level, it rises from a slightly raised level as its structures on the street clearly witness. Built between 128 and 138 A.D., it soared for three or four stories. (The front stairway gives proof of up to three floors.)

The right side of the first floor facing the House of Diana (59) was made up of shops and mezzanines; the left side, instead, of splendid eight- to ten-room apartments with refined wall decorations of which the Insula of Jupiter and Ganymede (61) is a valid example. The utilization of the building was completed by commercial premises on the north side, among which was a deposit of *dolii* for oil or wine. The court that the airy, triple-opening mullioned windows of the rich apartments overlooked was decorated with a polychrome mosaic representing allegorical figures of the months. It is presumable that these prestigious apartment buildings were inhabited by that class of wealthy merchants or high state officials who for professional reasons were forced to gravitate around the harbor zone.

65. **Cardo Maximus**
67. **Via Tecta**
68. **Small Market**

Like all of the contiguous constructions, the buildings facing the Cardoo Maximus (65), street perpendicular to the Decumanus Maximus, also were reconstructed and enlarged by Hadrian in 120 A.D.

(Above) Apartment Building of the Dolii. Warehouse.
(Below) Insula of Jupiter and Ganymede. Southeast side.

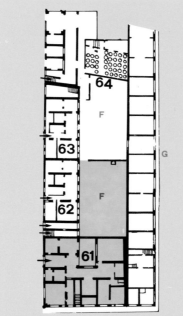

APARTMENT BUILDING
61 - Insula of Jupiter and Ganymede
62 - Insula of the Child Bacchus
63 - Insula of the Paintings
64 - Warehouse of the Dolii
F - Court
G - Taverns.
Blue - Mosaic

The wide avenue which began behind the imposing *Capitolium* was flanked by two long arcades that held shops while living quarters were on the upper floors.

To its left runs a short parallel street called Via Tecta (67) where tombstones and votive cippi regarding the life of Ostia's ancient inhabitants were gathered and inventoried.

Adjacent to the Via Tecta is the porticoed court of a large *horrea* called Small Market (68). It is a warehouse in fairly good condition. The vaults of the cells on the south side were restored during the 1938 excavations in order to have large-capacity premises for holding archaeological findings. The Small Market incorporates into its structures a large part of the *castrum*'s old walls in *opus quadratum*, still visible from the small external street. In one of the warehouse cells is preserved a medieval lime furnace used for burning marble.

69. Curia
70. Apartment Building of the Lararium

The curia, seat of Ostia's senate, was the public building that, together with the basilica, represented the center of the city's political-forensic life. Little or nothing remains of it. The building's perimetrical brick wall leads one to suppose that it was faced with marble slabs. The Apartment Building of the Lararium, dating around 125 A.D., is a particularly interesting building from the point of view of its utilization. An entrance led from the street into a quadrangular court where, a singular case, shops with mezzanines open onto it one after another. This way of gathering so many shops together in one place makes it presumable that they were probably specialized in the sale of like merchandise of a certain value. It was probably a corporation of craftsmen who sold jewels.

(Above) Small Market Horrea. Storage rooms.
(Below) Apartment Building of the Lararium. Interior.

71. Domus of the Round Temple
72. Basilica
73. Round Temple

Lovely rich *domus* (71) of the II-III century A.D., it preserves traces of mosaic flooring in some rooms and in the portico there is a well preserved columnar peristyle enriched by a decorative pond.

Almost nothing remains of the basilica (72), fulcrum of the public and forensic life. Probably, as the modest surviving fragments lead to believe, the building was rich in marble to which recourse was indiscriminately made during all of the Middle Ages in order to make lime out of it. Traces of the marble floor and an arch of the portico along the forum where bas-reliefs representing putti holding up floral festoons stand out are enough to give us an idea of the stateliness of this building.

Adjacent to the basilica is the grandiose Round Temple (73) from the III century A.D. whose dome soared in front of an immense peristyle capable of holding a large crowd during religious ceremonies. Probably dedicated to the cult of deified emperors, when it was discovered in 1800 it offered innumerable sculptures and portraits of persons belonging to the imperial families.

75. Domus of Jupiter the Fulminator

This is one of the *domus* in Ostia that has undergone innumerable restorations and remodelling throughout several centuries. Dated 65-78 A.D., it offers a curiosity: the seals impressed on the bricks of its walls belonged to the furnace of a certain L. Iulius Lesbius who at the same time contributed with his bricks toward the construction of several buildings in Pompeii and to the building of the Colosseum in Rome.

Domus of the Round Temple. Interior.
Tavern of the Fishmongers. Selling counter.

ROUND TEMPLE
Reconstructed vertical section

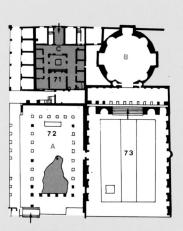

A - Basilica
B - Round Temple
C - Domus of the Round Temple

Blue - Mosaic

78. Macellum
79. Taverns
of the Fishmongers

Paved in marble with a gutter for draining dirty water away and decorated with a pretty central fountain which provided a continuous, abundant jet of water: this must have been the clean, refreshing image presented by the *Macellum* (78), Ostia's market for meats and other foodstuffs. Towards the back of it, a high columnar podium may have held a display of goods. One can imagine that like all city markets it was always crowded with shouting people if some witty fellow of the day, almost as if wanting to justify this phenomenon, on one of the podium's columns wrote the phrase, "*Read and know that a lot of chattering goes on in the market place*".

The *Macellum* communicates with two taverns called "of the Fishmongers" (79) which were embellished with fine marble counters and some basins containing live fish.

Both the Macellum and the Taverns of the Fishmongers date back to the end of the I-beginning of the II century A.D., but they had numerous restorations which document their long life, protracted for certain up to the V century A.D.

80. Insula of Dionysus
81. Insula of the Eagle
82. Mithraeum
of the Seven Doors
83. Baths
of the Six Columns

Beyond the Taverns of the Fishmongers (79) along the Decumanus Maximus, two *insulae* are set side by side; the *Insula* of Dionysus (80) and the *Insula* of the Eagle (81). Both of them built in 125-130 A.D., Hadrian's epoch, they were restored and partly modified around the middle of the III century and this late remodelling considerably changed the face of the old *insulae*. Inside, several mosaics and frescoes show the considerable refinement of their decoration.

In a room at the rear of the *Insula* of the Eagle is preserved the *Mithraeum* of the Seven Doors (82) which boasts a fresco representing a lovely garden.

The *insulae* are next to the baths called "of the Six Columns" (83) of which the *frigidarium* and the pools of the *calidarium* are still well preserved.

84. Schola of Trajan

A lovely marble-paved exedra originally adorned with columns and statues was the sumptuous entrance to this collegial seat which rose in the II century A.D. in the space where precedently a *domus* with atrium and peristyle had been built. The building encloses a spacious internal porticoed court in which a long pool lies. In back, a room from a later epoch presents an airy triclinium with spiral columns and a fine black and white mosaic. On the left side of the court, a brief tract of the peristyle of the I century B.C. *domus* has been reconstructed. Of considerable interest is the room of the *domus* paved in mosaic and reproducing a geometric composition with small tesserae, rare, precious example of the mosaic technique during the republican period.

The statue of the emperor Trajan in breast plate was found in the *schola* (the original is in the museum). That has led to presume that the *schola* belonged to the corporation of the shipbuilders who particularly venerated Trajan, author of the expansion of the port and naval yards of which the shipbuilders were the direct beneficiaries.

86. Portico of the Oil-lamp Fountain

The long building with columnar portico that lines the Decumanus Maximus almost as far as the Marine Gate takes its name from the graceful marble fountain on the street. Built in 125 A.D., this large edifice had shops under the porticoes on the first floor and living quarters on the upper floors. It was built on top of a precedent porticoed building of which a brief tract is still visible along the Decumanus, evidenced by a cement covering.

87. Caupona of Alexander Helix

SCHOLA OF THE TRAJAN
F - Hall of the Trajan's Statue
G - Domus of the I century B.C

Blue - Mosaic

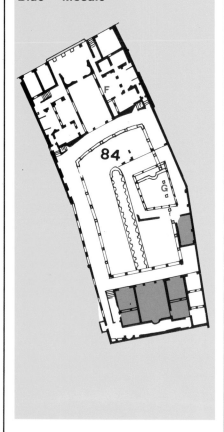

(Above) Schola of Trajan. Court with fountain.
(Below) Apartment Building of the Oil Lamp Fountain. Fountain.

(Left) Marine Gate. Remains of the gate and entrance to the Caupona of Alexander Helix.
(Right) Sepulchral monument of Cartilius Poplicola.

88. Marine Gate

The Marine Gate was the city gate that looked onto the seacoast, then little more than a hundred meters away. A few blocks of tufa and traces of the antique flagstones remain of it. The fortified walls built by Sulla in 79 B.C. were not enough to hold back the pirate attacks carried out by the Cilicians in 67 B.C. which brought destruction to the Roman fleet anchored in Ostia's harbor besides causing considerable damage to civil constructions. Both the walls and the gates underwent restorations around the beginning of the I century A.D., but little more than one hundred years later, at the time of Hadrian (120 A.D.), those same walls were rendered useless by the inhabitants of Ostia themselves who set private and public buildings on top of them in an urban growth which by that time was protected by the impressive Roman military expansion which had carried the empire's frontiers to much more distant shores.

One of the two towers that flanked the gate was even occupied in the second half of the II century A.D. by a tavern called *Caupona* of Alexander Helix (87) from the name written in mosaic on the floor. This tavern which appears to have been restored in the III century A.D. has a counter for serving wine and a small basin still in good condition. The floor's mosaic illustrates three distinct scenes. There are a Venus with cupid, two wrestlers in the bold act of fighting, and two dancers, illustrations which allow one to imagine the tastes of the *caupona*'s customers. The two dancers in that grotesque posture remind one of the ancient Egyptian dances; that, together with other findings discovered in the city, would confirm the presence of an oriental community in Ostia.

89. Sepulchral Monument
90. Sanctuary of the Good Goddess
91. Lightning-Struck Domus
92. Tomb
of Cartilius Poplicola
95. Domus

Beyond the Marine Gate, we find a group of mixed constructions which can confuse the visitor. It is certain that ever since the construction of the Sullan Wall, this part of the city outside the gate was set aside, as were the areas just outside of the other gates for that matter, as burial ground for the dead; the two sepulchral monuments (89, 92) towering above the area are proof of it. But the zone that looked directly onto the beach must have been too beautiful and inviting to save exclusively for that sad use; so already at the end of the I century A.D. two lovely *domus* (91, 95) and a temple dedicated to the Good Goddess (90) had been raised along the continuation of the Decumanus outside of the gate. Other more imposing constructions were added in the II century such as the charming forum directly to the left of the gate and a series of buildings for use as shops and living quarters. The large Baths of Marciana (93) were raised and another imposing porticoed building called Sea Front which represents the extreme extension of the city's building in the beach's direction. Here in the 1960's following excavations for laying out some parking space along the modern road, a grandiose example of *opus sectile* was found which is without doubt the most qualifying work of art discovered during the city's excavation. In this arabesque marble work dating back to the late empire, the craft of the carvers of that epoch was magistrally exalted in splendid figurations. Among other things, there is a bearded man rendered in the act of giving the benediction who is said to represent Christ. Part of this work of art, now restored, is on display in Ostia's museum.

Of the two *domus* along the road, certainly the more interesting is the Lightning-Struck *Domus* (91), thus named after the discovery of a small tumulus which records that tragic event. It boasts an external triclinium built in the peristyle of the house, rare example in Ostia.

The various buildings and the subsequent restorations and enlargements carried out during the late empire have purposely saved the two sepulchral monuments, revealing in this way the veneration that Ostia's ancient inhabitants nurtured for those two ancient personages.

The apsed sepulchral monument immediately outside the Marine Gate (89) was built about 30 B.C. Constructed wholly in travertine, it reveals a valuable facing. A fine Roman ship rostrum leads to believe it may have belonged to some important man of sea from Ostia.

Noteworthy is the sepulchral monument belonging to C. Cartilius Poplicola, high political-military personage of Ostia who lived in the second half of the I century B.C. Several inscriptions found during excavations of Ostia speak of him. The sixteen lictor fasces framing the inscription on the right side of the monument document his repeated victories in elections for the title of city duumvir. The monument's frieze illustrates his participation in some important war event, rendered synthetically by a trireme and some soldiers in fighting trim.

93. Baths of the Marciana

The thermae extend along the Via Severiana within a few meters of the sea. Laid out over a precedent construction, they were built at the end of the II century A.D. The fine brick construction offers the visitor a still vibrant image of its ancient stateliness.

The large room that held the *frigidarium*, of which two pillars of the apse of a pool remain as mighty witnesses, measured over 14 meters per side. In a small adjacent room which was perhaps a dressing room (*apodytherium*), a magnificent black and white mosaic recently came to light wherein with refined skill athletes are represented in poses that mirror the various sport disciplines of the time; athletic apparatus, weapons, and trophies are at the mosaic's center. The southwest side of the building facing the Via Severiana is occupied by the *calidarium* system.

The edifice was repeatedly restored even beyond the V century.

In the last few years, several excavations near the synagogue in the vicinity of the thermae have brought other imposing buildings back to light which demonstrate the city's expansion outside of the city wall and along the coastline.

94. Synagogue

Discovered during trial excavations carried out in 1961, the synagogue was built in the I century A.D. between the Via Severiana and the beach of ancient times and underwent innumerable readaptations and restorations until after the IV century A.D. Decorated in a late epoch with four columns with composite capitals, it still offers traces of mosaic flooring. In the large hall, an apsed tabernacle shows two small columns that held corbels reproducing seven-branched candelabra. The ark with the Torah was kept there. An adjacent hall is furnished with a counter and an oven, probably the place where the unleavened bread was prepared.

P. 42 Sepulchral monument.
(Above left) Baths of the Marciana. Remains of the apse of the frigidarium.
(Below left) Baths of the Marciana. Mosaic of athletes.
(Above right) Synagogue. Corbels with candelabra.
(Below right) Synagogue. General view.

96. Domus of the Nymphaeum

Next to the *Domus* of the Dioscuri rises the pretty triple-opening mullioned window of the IV century A.D. *Domus* of the *Nymphaeum*. It preserves a *Nymphaeum* which in ancient times held statues in its niches and a pleasant water display animated by graceful marble glides. The marble floor in *opus sectile* is of interest.

This is a grand, rich residential complex whose functionality and avantgarde architectonic planning distinguish it from all of Ostia's residences. Built at the time of Hadrian (125 A.D.), it seems to demonstrate the change in taste and living aspirations that had taken place among Ostia's wealthy ancient inhabitants. Perhaps owning a rich *domus* with atrium and peristyle enclosed by

A - Insula of the Muses
B - Insula of the Yellow Walls
    Insula of the Graffito
C - Taverns
D - Insula of the Dioscuri
F - Main entrance to the Garden
    Homes

Blue - Mosaic

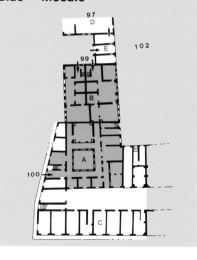

(Above) Domus of the Nymphaeum. The triple-opening mullioned window.
(Centre) Insula of the Muses. Decoration of a room.
(Below) Insula of the Muses. Main entrance.
P. 45 (Above) Domus of the Dioscuri. Polychrome mosaic of the large room.
P. 45 (Below) Domus of the Dioscuri. Polychrome mosaic of a room.
P. 45 (Below right) Domus of the Dioscuri. Nereid riding a sea monster. Detail.

heavy walls that isolated it was too costly or else it represented an outdated style. It seems clear that in this historical period Ostia is embellished by these residential complexes composed of rich *insulae* having large, airy single- and double-opening mullioned windows overlooking a condominial garden for which the wealthy owners or renters willingly divided maintenance costs. Black and white mosaics reproducing geometric motifs with charming effects of perspective and delicate wall frescoes where light panels frame colored birds and small squares or figures decorate these *insulae*. It is without doubt the evolution of a city rich in commerce and cultural exchange that pushes even the well-to-do towards a socialization among neighbours which cannot be found in any other place at that time.

Of these splendid *insulae*, the only one that still may be visited now (the others are closed to visitors) is that on the south side called *Domus* of the Dioscuri (97) which underwent important modifications and restorations, however, that completely changed its decoration in the late empire. Still noteworthy is the great polychrome mosaic of the IV century reproducing Tritons and Nereids in imitation of the II century Roman bath mosaics. In the small adjacent rooms, other polychrome mosaics decorate the *domus*. A small private Roman bath demonstrates the affluence of these late owners, who made something unique and unrepeatable of the various *domus* of the IV century.

101. Insula of the Painted Vaults

Built at the time of Hadrian and restored in a later epoch, it presents some interesting and disconcerting aspects. It rises two stories high. The first floor seems divided lengthwise by a narrow corridor off of which small rooms open. A tavern with a fine counter occupies the north corner of the building. A very well preserved staircase on the northeast side leads to the second floor where one may note a room used as a kitchen still in perfect condition with a very well preserved counter with stove. A pipe for waste water laid against the window that lighted the kitchen reveals the system's functionality. A small rectangular room plastered with crushed potsherd which looks like a water tank or a tub for bathing completes the service area. Other anonymous rooms with traces of fresco decorations take up all of the rest of the second floor.

Later restorations transformed the *insula* into a *lupanare* (house of pleasure); wall paintings and graffiti bear witness to it. This seems a little disconcerting, considering that the building is in the part of Ostia that has the greatest number of prestigious homes. It seems strange, in fact, that the inhabitants of those sumptuous *insulae* surrounding the building did not object to the continuous coming and going of the house's noisy, bold customers.

103. Maritime Baths

Edifice for Roman baths dating back to the Hadrian period, it incorporates a tract of the Sullan Wall into its structures. Several black and white mosaics representing sea divinities are interesting.

105. Temple of the Shipbuilders

Built in an area enclosed by the Corporation of Shipbuilders of Ostia, the temple dates back to the III century A.D. Within the complex that holds it, 43 roughly hewed columns

and several capitals were found during the excavation and they are still lying there. It is presumable that this material was stacked during the late empire in anticipation of restorations and enlargements and then for some reason was abandoned.

(Above) Insula of the Painted Vaults. Southwest side of the building.
(Below) Christian Basilica. Interior.

(Above) House of Serapis. Panoramic view.
(Below) Baths of the Seven Sages. Circular room.

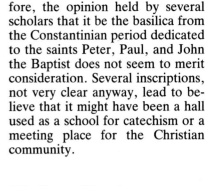

106. Christian Basilica

The place was made by modifying and adapting some areas of the adjacent Roman bath building which dates back to the late empire. Therefore, the opinion held by several scholars that it be the basilica from the Constantinian period dedicated to the saints Peter, Paul, and John the Baptist does not seem to merit consideration. Several inscriptions, not very clear anyway, lead to believe that it might have been a hall used as a school for catechism or a meeting place for the Christian community.

108. House of Serapis

Of this fine building built by Hadrian in 120 A.D. rests the porticoed court with its pillars still stuccoed. A staircase on the left of the portico leads to the second floor where from a terrace it is now possible to enjoy an excellent panoramic view of the city and a tract of the Tiber River which flows not far away. One goes from the portico to the Baths of the Seven Sages (109).

109. Baths of the Seven Sages

Having crossed the portico of the House of Serapis (108), one enters the Roman bath complex called "of the Seven Sages". Opening on the left side is a great circular hall, vaulted in ancient times. Traces showing where the coffers were embedded are still visible on the north side. A great black and white mosaic representing hunting scenes paves the hall.

An arch still bearing traces of polychrome vitreous paste brings us into a vestibule adjacent the pool. On the walls here are still well preserved frescoes representing the seven sages with, beside them, their names and advice in very frank language on how to keep the body functioning well.

On the side opposite the circular hall, there is a *laconicum* for steam baths and the *calidarium*; on the right, a pool with a lovely fresco representing an Aphrodite bathing in a sea full of fish of every kind.

Heading south, one comes to the adjoining House of the Charioteers (110).

110. House of the Charioteers
111. Chapel
of the Three Aisles

This large apartment building gets its name from two charioteers frescoed in the corridor on its first floor. It is, along with the contiguous Baths of the Seven Sages (109) and the House of Serapis (108), one of the highest ruins in the city. The piers with arches that delimit the court, over ten meters high, give us an idea of how the three story building appeared.
Built around 120 A.D. by Hadrian, it clearly represents a leap in the evolution of Ostia's average home. Physically attached to the Baths of the Seven Sages and the House of Serapis, it also includes a temple called Chapel of the Three Aisles (111), perhaps a *mithraeum* reserved for worship by those living in the apartment building. Some scholars have seen in this clustering, composed of homes with shops, thermae, and temple, an example of a self-sufficient living complex.

112. House of Annius

Edifice dated 128 A.D., it still has some fairly well preserved frescoes in several rooms. On the southwest side of the house under the vaults of the balcony, a clay tablet states its owner's name.

113. Baths of Trinacria
114. Apartment building of Serapis
Apartment building
of Bacchus and Ariadne

A small narrow street leads into a particularly interesting complex composed of the Baths of Trinacria and a fine apartment building built in the Hadrian period. The latter, which is set against a partially excavated large provisions warehouse, is composed of a living nucleus called the House of Bacchus and Ariadne and of a small temple dedicated to Jovi Serapidi.
The position of the thermae (113) leads to believe that they were reserved for the personnel that gravitated in the area of the great ware-

houses, thus porters, port laborers, merchants, as well as those who lived in the apartment building.
The House of Bacchus and Ariadne, which takes up two floors, still has its mosaic flooring on the first floor. These mosaics, along with others dated between 120-130 A.D., are among the most significative of Ostia. Both for the originality of the design's layout and for the stylization of the floral motifs, the black and white mosaic of the triclinium

which reproduces the struggle between Cupid and Pan or sacred and profane love in the presence of Dionysus and Ariadne is the most beautiful of the house. The figures in the central field framed by vine leaves and tendrils reveal the refined taste and the advanced evolution that Ostia's mosaic art had reached. The floor has the figures facing the end of the room where it is supposed the host sat among his table companions.

To the side of the House of Bacchus and Ariadne stands the temple of Jovi Serapidi, divinity of the Egyptian-Hellenistic civilization. The entrance's black and white mosaic floor reproduces the bull Apis. The now bare temple reveals traces of successive restorations. To the left of the temple in a beautiful quadrangular room which perhaps was the priest's home or a place for reunions, there is a polychrome mosaic reproducing scenes of the Nile and exotic animals in small panels.

P. 48 House of the Charioteers. Portico.
(Above) House of the Charioteers. Remains of the building.
(Below) House of Annius. Façade.
(Right) Mosaic of Bacchus and Ariadne. Detail.

A college that gathered together those in charge of controlling and measuring wheat found its ufficial seat in the building that was incorporated into this great *horrea*. The hall holding the fine mosaic of the *mensores* must have been the place for weighing grain of the college named Corpus mensorum frumentariorum ostiensium. Their activity is very well illustrated by the mosaic itself. The *mensores* with the *rutellum* measured the amount of wheat while two other individuals controlled the quality and humidity of the wheat itself; the boy, it seems, was in charge of counting the sacks. Two porters complete the scene.

Adjacent the *Horrea* of the Wheat Measurers, another large *horrea* called the Trajan Markets (117) can be seen. Although only partially excavated, it is possible to see part of their great vaults, still intact. It is thought that these, together with the *Horrea* of the Wheat Measurers, were reserved exclusively for grain.

Not far away over the unexplored dunes extends the complex that was called Imperial Palace (115, 116) which included a building for Roman baths and a *mithraeum* dating back to the middle of the II century A.D.

120. Baths of Mithra

Built in 125 A.D., they underwent considerable restorations and modernizing around 200 A.D. The building for Roman baths, in excellent condition in the underground part where the service corridors branch off, offers us some very suggestive views. A system for lifting water (noria) is visible in the corridor where the steps are. Marks cut into a wall of the

TEMPLE OF HERCULES
Reconstructed façade

deep, narrow room have been left by the large wheel furnished with pails that lifted the water up to the small cistern above it. From here, the water was conveyed through lead tubes into the pools or boilers. In the summer months when infiltration waters leave those underground areas dry, it is possible to admire the *mithraeum* made out of the cistern room which was already in disuse in ancient times and an industrial plant, perhaps a laundry and dye-shop, made at the rear of that. The very beautiful marble group of the god Mithra killing the bull, now kept in the museum, comes from this underground *mithraeum*.

121. Sacred Area of the Republican Temples

It includes in a trapezoidal area the great Temple of Hercules Invictus and another two smaller temples whose divinities are not known. Built at the time of Sulla in blocks of

tufa, they emerge from the old level of the republican city. Still standing now are the high *podia* and part of the cell walls. All three temples underwent numerous restorations and remodelling beginning in 112 A.D., Trajan's epoch, to which are dated the restorations of the brick built cell in the Temple of Hercules. Other restorations followed one after the other between the IV and V centuries A.D., thanks to the emperors Theodosius and Arcadius. These last late restorations document the fondness and devotion that Ostia's ancient inhabitants had for this very antique pagan cult. On the south side of the sacred area flanking the Via della Foce, a modest system for the filtration and purification of water from a well had been made in a room from a later epoch. That, together with the many other wells dug in what were even then ancient apartment buildings, in the *domus*, and along the city's very streets, witnesses that Ostia's poor population during the V or VI century A.D., when the city

was already left without its own aqueduct, perhaps destroyed following invasions or from lack of restorations, was forced to drink the salty water that was found a few centimeters beneath the level of the republican city.

122. Domus of Cupid and Psyche

This is one of the many *domus* that were built in the IV century A.D. and that reveal a particular richness in their decoration. Notable for its stateliness is the great columnar *nymphaeum* which one notes upon entering the house. Several small rooms facing the *nymphaeum* have walls decorated with polychrome marble; in one of them, the copy of the marble group representing Cupid and Psyche stands out (the original is in the museum). The triclinium, also faced with valuable marbles, has a splendid polychrome floor in *opus sectile*.
It is thought that most of these late *domus* built in Ostia belonged to the wealthy merchants whose business was connected with maritime trade, but who preferred to remain in Ostia rather than move to the tumultuous, heavily populated Portus.

123. Baths of Buticosus

Constructed in 112 A.D., Trajan's epoch, they are composed of various rooms showing traces of fresco painting. They get their name from the mosaic representing a bath attendant, Buticosus, portrayed on the floor of the room that precedes the *laconicum*. In fairly good condition is the *calidarium* where a fine mosaic representing a scene with sea divinities stands out between two small marble-faced pools.

P. 50 Domus of Cupid and Psyche. Nymphaeum.
Baths of Buticosus. Calidarium.

124. Epagathian and Epafroditian Horrea

This stately apartment building with porticoed court was used by its owners Epagathius and Epafroditius as a warehouse. This is one of the rare *horrea* in Ostia whose owners are known, their names being conspicuously written on the tablet set in the tympanum of the main entrance.

Dating back to the II century A.D., it was presumably used as an emporium since the inside rooms looking onto the porticoed court present several construction expedients which differ quite a bit from those of other *horrea*. In fairly good condition as far up as the middle of the second floor, it has several shops on the front and a fine entrance with a vestibule having brick semi-columns. Inside, the quadrangular court is floored in black and white mosaic in whose center is an emblem with a prominent swastika (crooked cross), considered in those days a magical symbol against bad luck. The inside rooms, well preserved and having their cross vaults still intact, are presently used as magazines for archaeological findings discovered during excavations.

(Above) Epagathian Horrea. Remains of the building.
(Below) Epagathian Horrea. Main Entrance.

PORTUS OSTIAE

Port of Claudius (after an antique print).

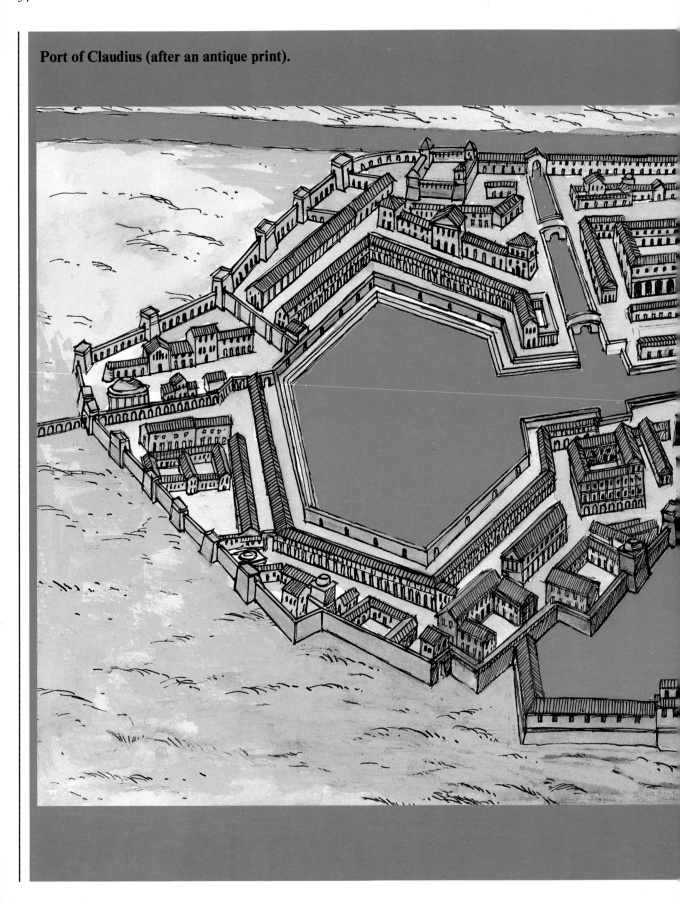

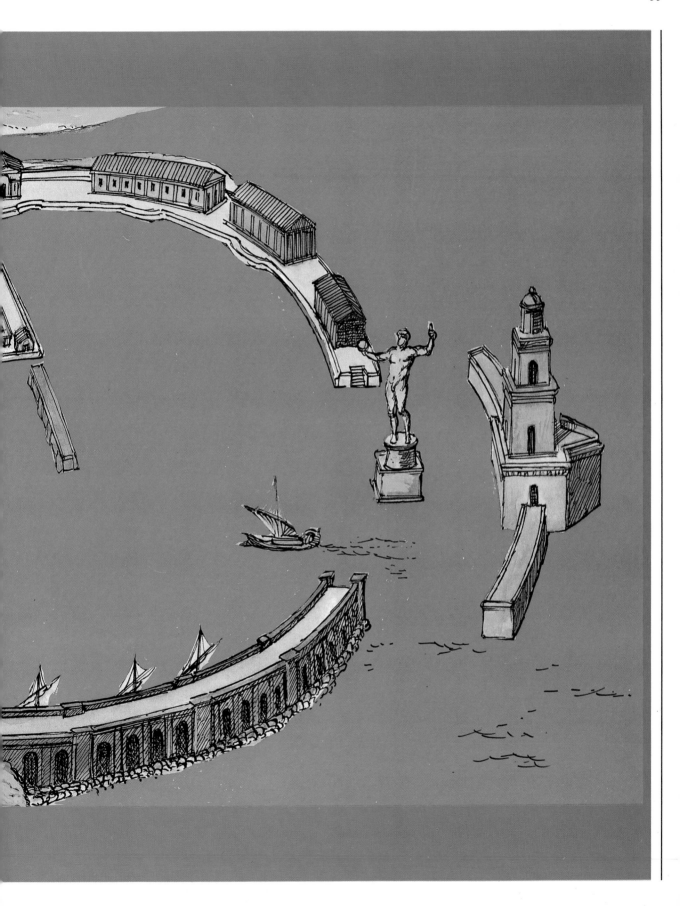

PORTUS OSTIAE

That Ostia had a rather insufficient harbor appears from innumerable ancient witnesses. Despite suppositions, nothing whatsoever has ever been found of it which by giving evidence of its port structures might establish the exact point in which it was situated. Very recent excavations done in the small town of Ostia (Antica) have brought to light an imposing structure in *opus quadratum* about one hundred meters long and ten wide that must be unequivocally identified as a fluvial wharf suitable for loading and unloading cargo.

This port fell into decline at least partially at the time of the emperor Claudius who wanted Ostia to have a port more in accordance with its trade, which was continuing to increase. Therefore, he built a great harbor basin to the northwest of the city along the littoral which was originally called portus Ostiae and portus Augusti. Concerning the construction of this quite challenging project, an event was told which was afterwards confirmed by recent excavations. The lighthouse that the emperor Claudius wanted rising from the sea at the harbor's entrance was set upon a small artificial island created by sinking, and filling with lime and tufa, the gigantic ship that had brought the monolithic obelisk from Egypt which was to decorate the central divider of the Vatican Circus and which now towers in the center of St. Peter's Square in Rome.

Inaugurated by Nero in 54 A.D., the port was enlarged by Trajan with the construction of an imposing hexagonal dock and by a canal dug in the hinterland (Trajan's Channel) which united it to the course of the Tiber, thus allowing fluvial traffic of goods up to Rome.

(Above) Port of Ostia. Remains of the wharf in the area of the Leonardo da Vinci Airport.
(Below) Port of Ostia. Image of the Lighthouse on an Architrave.

The lighthouse of the Port of Claudius.

The new port zone, so detached from the city, probably created logistic problems for those in charge of harbor traffic who lived in Ostia, and many of them considered it more practical and convenient to move warehouses and homes directly into its vicinity. If this transfer was extremely slow, it nonetheless was a sure cause of the formation of a large inhabited area that increasingly gravitated around the new port. Having thus very slowly become a city apart, at the time of Constantine the Portus Ostiae was assigned all of the municipal rights that Ostia had held and was given the title of Civitas Constantiniana. The port was no longer Portus Ostiae, but Portus Romae. That caused the slow but constant decline of Ostia and its rich commerce.

At the present time, a tract of the wharf of the Port of Claudius is visible in the zone of the Leonardo da Vinci Airport in Fiumicino. The part of it comprising the hexagonal dock built by Trajan and all of the relative port structures are closed within private property and thus can not be visited. Of the Portus Romae, several fragments of Roman cargo ships remain which are kept in a museum built on the very site where they were found (in the area of the airport).

Little or nothing has been handed down concerning daily life in the city of Portus. Some excavations carried out at the beginning of the century have made it possible to identify several large, mighty port structures as well as ruins of warehouses used for stowage of goods. In the 1930's, in the Isola Sacra area along the Via Flavia which connected Portus with Ostia, its necropolis was brought to light, wonderfully preserved by the littoral sands that had completely buried it during the centuries. In this way, it was also hidden from the feared tomb profaners of the Middle Ages, so that during the excavation it proved to be rich in very valuable findings.

The tombs, almost all of which still appear in magnificent condition, are dated between the I and III century A.D. Built singly, they stand side by side. The façades and the tympanums overhanging them are in brick with architectonic decorations obtained by cutting into the bricks themselves. Barrel vaults cover the cells where, indifferently, ashes from cremation and sarcophagi for inhumation were placed.

Surrounding these quite prestigious tombs, one may note graves, trunk-style tombs, little temples, and a cemetery for the poor. Among the curiosities, an Egyptian tomb built in brick, reproducing a pyramid in miniature.

Funeral inscriptions and clay tablets representing artisans' trades placed on the tombs tell about the life of the inhabitants of Portus. The number of freedmen (slaves set free) who exercised various trades is considerable.

Despite all of these findings, nothing had yet been found which might document a city surrounding the port. In the years 1960-61, with the construction of a road linking Ostia to the airport in Fiumicino, some trial excavations led to the discovery of parts of buildings which were evidence of that imposing city which was the Civitas Costantiniana. Traces of imposing buildings for Roman baths, homes, and ancient industrial plants appeared along the canal of Fiumicino (Trajan's Channel), as well as streets lined with taverns and public buildings. At the foot of the necropolis in the zone called "dell'Opera Nazionale Combattenti", findings from the late empire came to light and, among them, the antique basilica of St. Hippolytus. A bell tower dating back to the XI-XII century built right next to the ancient Christian basilica documents the continuity of Christian living, even though modest, perpetuated on the site throughout the entire Middle Ages.

Port of Claudius.

Ostia Antique.
Design.
By courtesy
of the
Editori Romani
Associati.

GLOSSARY

APODYTERIUM – Dressing room in the thermae.

ARCOSOLIUM – Arched niche for placing sarcophagus.

ATRIUM – Hall or court of a Roman villa.

AUGUSTALES – Those in charge of the cult of deified emperors.

AUGUSTEUM – Place of worship dedicated to the cult of emperors.

CALIDARIUM – Room in the thermae having hot water pools.

CAPITOLIUM – Temple dedicated to Jupiter, Juno, and Minerva.

CARDO MAXIMUS – Main street (crosswise) of the Roman city.

CARRUCA – Ancient four-wheeled cart.

CASTRUM – Fortified citadel; originally, Roman soldiers' encampment.

CAUPONA – Ancient tavern.

CISIARII – Cart drivers.

CISIUM – Ancient carriage for passengers.

COLLEGE or CORPORATION – Trade association.

COLUMBARIUM – Tomb having niches in its walls wherein terracotta containers holding the dead's ashes were placed.

CURIA – Meeting place for the local senate.

DECUMANUS MAXIMUS – Main street (lengthwise) of the Roman city.

DOLII – Large terra-cotta jars.

DOMUS – Roman villa.

DUUMVIR – Roman magistrate.

FORICA – Latrine.

FORNIX – Arched entrance.

FRIGIDARIUM – Room in the thermae having cold water pools.

FULLONICA – Laundry and dye-shop.

HORREA – Warehouse for storing commodities.

INSULA – Apartment in an apartment building.

LACONICUM – Room in the thermae for taking steam baths.

LARARIUM – Home Lar oratory.

MACELLUM – Food market.

MENSORES – Those in charge of measuring grain.

MITHRA – God worshipped under Mithraism, oriental mystery cult.

MITHRAEUM – Mithraist temple.

MULLION – Slender column dividing the lights or openings of a window.

NYMPHAEUM – Water displays dedicated to nymphs; fountain.

OPUS QUADRATUM – Building technique used in the republican age.

OPUS SECTILE – Marble inlay.

PEDIMENT – Architectonic element which includes the whole of the architrave, frieze, and cornice.

PERISTYLE – Porticoed court.

PODIUM – Platform; bench.

RUTELLUM – Rule for leveling grain in the bushel.

SACELLUM – Chapel.

SCHOLA – Seat of a college or corporation.

SERAPEUM – Temple dedicated to Serapis.

SODALES – Members of a college.

SUSPENSURAE – Square brick pillars placed under the floor which allowed warm air to circulate.

THERMAE – Edifice for public Roman baths.

THERMOPOLIUM – Ancient tavern.

TRUNK-STYLE TOMB – Brick tomb having the rounded upper part above ground level.

BIBLIOGRAPHY